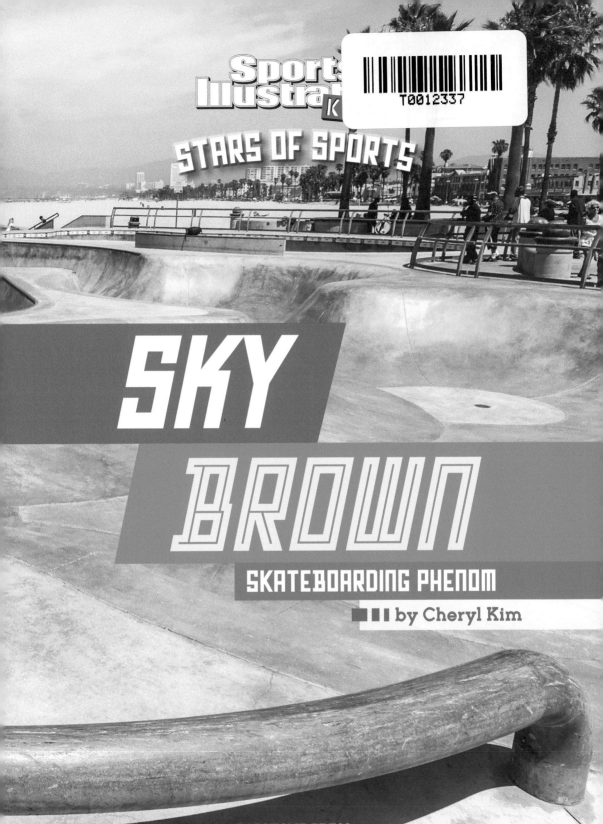

Sports Illustrated Kids

STARS OF SPORTS

SKY BROWN

SKATEBOARDING PHENOM

■■■ by Cheryl Kim

CAPSTONE PRESS
a capstone imprint

Published by Capstone Editions, an imprint of Capstone
1710 Roe Crest Drive, North Mankato, Minnesota 56003
capstonepub.com

SPORTS ILLUSTRATED KIDS is a trademark of ABG-SI LLC. Used with permission.

Library of Congress Cataloging-in-Publication Data
Names: Kim, Cheryl, author. Title: Sky Brown : skateboarding phenom / by Cheryl Kim.
Description: North Mankato, Minnesota : Capstone Press, 2022. | Series: Sports illustrated kids stars of sports | Includes
bibliographical references and index. | Audience: Ages 8-11 | Audience: Grades 4-6 | Summary: "At just 10 years of age,
Sky Brown became the youngest professional skateboarder in the world. Instead of using a coach, she learns her tricks
online. She's not afraid to take risks and push limits. After a horrific fall left her unresponsive with several skull fractures
and a broken left hand and wrist, Brown is still determined to be the best skateboarder in the world!"— Provided by publisher.
Identifiers: LCCN 2021021007 (print) | LCCN 2021021008 (ebook) | ISBN 9781663983572 (hardcover) | ISBN 9781666323436
(paperback) | ISBN 9781666323443 (pdf) | ISBN 9781666323467 (kindle edition) Subjects: LCSH: Brown, Sky—Juvenile
literature. | Skateboarders—Biography—Juvenile literature. | Skateboarding—Juvenile literature. Classification: LCC GV859.813.
B76 K56 2022 (print) | LCC GV859.813.B76 (ebook) | DDC 796.22092 [B]—dc23 LC record available at https://lccn.loc.
gov/2021021007 LC ebook record available at https://lccn.loc.gov/2021021008

Editorial Credits
Editor: Christianne Jones; Designer: Bobbie Nuytten; Media Researcher: Morgan Walters; Production Specialist: Laura Manthe

Image Credits
Associated Press: Alexander Scheuber, 20, Charlie Neibergall, 19, KYDPL KYODO, 13, 23, Peter Byrne, 8; Getty Images:
BEHROUZ MEHRI, 26, CARL DE SOUZA, 24, Mel Melcon, 11, Rick Loomis, 15, Sean M. Haffey, 5; Newscom: Byron Purvis/
AdMedia, 9, Ian Cheibub/Reuters, Cover, 28; Shutterstock: nito, 17, trekandshoot, 1, Wilson Chu Wai Shun, 7

Source Notes
Page 4, "I just want to…," Michelle Bruton, "11-year-old skateboarder Sky Brown has shred cred beyond her years," TieBreaker,
September 10, 2019, https://www.tiebreaker.com, Accessed July 14, 2021.
Page 6, "It was my favorite…," Rick Maese, "She's 10 years old and loves to skateboard. She could be an Olympian next year,"
The Washington Post, June 21, 2019, https://www.washingtonpost.com, Accessed July 14, 2021.
Page 9, "She's really cool…," Sam Reed, "Her hopes of being Britain's youngest Olympian were dashed, So Sky Brown set the
bar higher," InStyle, April 24, 2020, https://www.instyle.com, Accessed July 14, 2021.
Page 10, "She skates bigger than…," Alice Truong, "An 8-year-old skateboarder became the youngest girl to compete against
adults at Vans' pro-competition," Quartz, September 17, 2016, https://qz.com, Accessed July 14, 2021.
Page 11, "Learning a new trick can…," (Clif Bar and Company,) "Sky Brown: The Biggest Little Thing to Hit the Deck,"
Clif Bar and Company, https://www.clifbar.com, Accessed July 14, 2021.
Page 12, Sky&Ocean, "10 year old wins huge skateboarding contest – Sky Brown travels to Estonia- Vlog#3 Simple Sessions,"
YouTube video, 7:45, February 25, 2019, https://www.youtube.com/watch?v=UcnViUoMz0w.
Page 14, Sky&Ocean, "Cambodian Diaries of a Skatergirl-Sky Brown," YouTube video, 2:34, October 25, 2017,
https://www.youtube.com/watch?v=vWPrpNEw8no.
Page 16, "Inspire other girls…," Colin Bane, "Q&A: Sky Brown Reflects on #3 World ranking, recovering from injury,
and Going huge," DewTour, https://www.dewtour.com, Accessed July 14, 2021.
Page 16, "If people see me…," Jonny Weeks, "Sky Brown, the 11-year-old Olympic hopeful: 'I want to push boundaries
for girls,'" The Guardian, December 11, 2019, https://www.theguardian.com, Accessed July 14, 2021.
Page 18, "I don't usually post…," Donald McRae, "Sky Brown: 'Sometimes you fall but I wanted to show me getting up again,'"
The Guardian, August 3, 2020, https://www.theguardian.com, Accessed July 14, 2021.
Page 21, "She could definitely be…," D'arcy Maine, "Tony Hawk calls Sky Brown 'a unicorn' on a skateboard," ESPN 5,
July 1, 2020, https://tv5.espn.com, Accessed July 14, 2021.
Page 22, "If they watch me…," Rick Maese, "She's 10 years old and loves to skateboard. She could be an Olympian next year,"
The Washington Post, June 21, 2019, https://www.washingtonpost.com, Accessed July 14, 2021.
Page 22, "The team GB proposition for Sky…," (Olympics,) "I want to show that it's not about your size or age," says
skateboard sensation Sky Brown," Olympics, January 13, 2020, https://olympics.com, Accessed July 14, 2021.

All internet sites appearing in back matter were available and accurate when this book was sent to press.

TABLE OF CONTENTS

Words in **BOLD** are in the glossary.

MAKING HISTORY

Balancing on the deck of her skateboard, 11-year-old Sky Brown launched herself off the edge of the Mega Ramp. Fans at ESPN's X Games Minneapolis 2019 held their breath. Brown grabbed her skateboard and rotated one and a half times in midair. She came down and nailed the landing! The audience cheered as Brown pumped her fists into the air. She had just made history as the first female to land a frontside 540 at the X Games!

Brown's run earned the young, 4-foot, 5-inch (135-centimeter) athlete fifth place. She couldn't stop smiling.

"I just want to be the little girl having fun and just doing these crazy tricks," Brown said.

FACT

Surfers invented the skateboard in the 1950s. They wanted to have the feeling of riding waves on land.

Brown focuses on one of her runs during the X Games in Minneapolis in 2019.

CHAPTER ONE

A SKATEBOARDING PRODIGY

Sky Brown was born in Miyazaki, Japan, on July 12, 2008. She has a British father and Japanese mother. Brown fell in love with skateboarding after watching her dad and his friends perform tricks on their backyard ramp. When she was about 3 years old, Brown borrowed her dad's skateboard to ride around the house.

"It was always my favorite toy," said Brown. "I'd just always want to play with it."

Brown begged her dad to teach her some skateboarding skills. He taught her a few tricks. Brown practiced them in her backyard and at her preschool's skate park. After learning **kick turns** on the ramp and **kickflips** with her board, Brown searched for new tricks online and began teaching herself.

>>> A picturesque view of
Japan's landscape, where
Brown was born.

Brown's dad uploaded skateboarding videos of Brown. One video had 50 million views within a few days! After that, event invitations came rolling in. Brown became known as a skateboarding **prodigy**.

Brown entered her first local contest at 7 years old. The contest was in California. Brown finished in third place.

》》》 An 11-year-old Sky Brown smiles for the cameras while sporting her Nike-sponsored gear in 2019.

> >>> Leticia Bufoni was one of Brown's role models in the skateboarding world.

Girl Power

Other female skateboarders like Leticia Bufoni inspired Brown to pursue professional skateboarding. Bufoni won five gold medals at the X Games. Brown said, "She doesn't care what people think . . . and she's really cool because sometimes girls think that if you do sport then you can't be a girly girl, but she's one. She has pink hair, she gets her nails done, she dresses up. I'm a girly girl too so I think she's really cool."

At the age of 8, Brown turned heads as the youngest skater at the 2016 Vans U.S. Open Pro Series. She wowed the crowd with her kickflips and **frontside 360**. Brown placed well even though she fell off her board during a **heat**. She finished higher than women twice her height and more than 20 years older.

"She skates bigger than her age," noted one reporter.

Brown has a few **signature** tricks. In the JAPAN AIR, she pulls the board up behind her back and grabs it while in the air. The Blunt Flip is when Brown flips her skateboard 360 degrees on the side of the ramp. Her Air Reverse Full Rotation is when Brown and her board make a full turn in the air. And in the frontside 540 Sky turns one and a half times in the air before landing on her board. The frontside 540 took the longest for Brown to learn.

"Learning a new trick can be a battle, but I love that feeling of winning the battle and getting a new trick. It's really addicting!" Brown said.

⟩⟩⟩ Sky Brown flips through the air while she practices tricks at a skate park in California.

FACT

The frontside 360 trick is a 360-degree rotation facing forward. In 2018, Brown was the first female to perform a frontside 720, which is two complete rotations facing forward.

FROM PRO TO PODIUM

In 2017, Brown traveled to Singapore to compete at the first-ever Vans Park Series in Asia. Brown took second place at the Continental Championships. This achievement brought her international recognition. Brown recalls placing at the competition as one of her proudest moments.

In 2019, Brown journeyed to Estonia to compete in the Simple Session. It was one of Europe's biggest skateboarding contests. It took place inside a giant arena with a huge obstacle course.

Brown said, "I'm a little nervous, but I'm just going to have fun and just go for it."

Brown finished in first place! That same year, she also placed first in the UK National Skateboarding Championship. She now ranked among the best skateboarders in the world.

>>> Brown shows off her bronze medal and skateboard at the World Championships.

CHAPTER THREE

SKATING FOR A CAUSE

Brown skates for causes she believes in. In 2019, she won the bronze medal at the World Park Skateboarding Championships in Brazil. Brown donated her prize money to the Make Life Skate Life foundation. This group helps build spaces to skate in communities and areas that wouldn't normally have them.

Brown also helped design a skateboard with the Almost Skateboards organization. The skateboard sales helped raise money for a nonprofit group called Skateistan. The group had just opened a new Skate School in Phnom Penh, Cambodia. Brown traveled there to teach children how to skate. Brown felt as if the children there taught her more than she taught them.

"They told me, 'We don't speak the same language, but it really doesn't matter. Inside we are the same. . . . We deserve to have hopes and dreams,'" Brown said.

>>> A member of the Skateistan organization teaches a young girl how to skateboard.

Skateistan

Skateistan is an organization that empowers children through skateboarding and education. The group focuses on children who are often left out from sports and educational opportunities. This includes girls, children living with disabilities, and those from low-income backgrounds.

POWERFUL PLATFORM

Brown lives six months of the year in Miyazaki, Japan, and the other six months in Oceanside, California, with her parents and younger brother, Ocean. No matter where she is, Brown stays connected with her hundreds of thousands of followers on social media. Brown shares videos of herself and her brother doing tricks, training, and vlogging about their everyday lives.

Most of all, Brown says she hopes her platform will "inspire other girls to have fun." In a sport traditionally thought of for boys, Brown is encouraging more girls to skate.

"If people see me, the smallest girl, doing the highest trick, then anyone could think they could do anything," said Brown.

>>> Venice Beach Skate Park is a famous skate park in California.

CHAPTER FOUR

GETTING BACK UP

In 2020, while training in California, Brown's board **veered** off the edge of the ramp. Brown fell almost 20 feet headfirst to the concrete floor. She put her left arm out to break the fall. Brown credits her helmet and arm for saving her life.

Brown fractured bones in her skull. She also broke bones in her left wrist and hand. She also injured her lungs and stomach. A helicopter airlifted her to the hospital. She arrived **unconscious** but made a miraculous recovery.

Brown decided to post the **footage** of that fall. In a video made from her hospital bed, Brown promised to keep going and train harder.

"I don't usually post my falls or talk about them because I want people to see the fun in what I do," said Brown. "But even if you're walking you can fall. So I thought it was good to show that sometimes you fall. But I also wanted to show me getting up."

>>> Sky Brown back from her injury competing in the Olympic qualifying event in 2021

>>> Brown and Tony Hawk pose
during the Laureus Sport for
Good skateboard event.

LESSONS FROM A LEGEND

Months after her fall, Brown was ready to get back to training. She reached out to her skateboarding mentor, Tony Hawk.

Tony said of Brown, "She could definitely be one of the best, well-rounded skaters ever, regardless of gender."

After the accident, Brown asked Tony to help her **conquer** professional skateboarder Elliot Sloan's 100-foot mega ramp. The ramp, which took three years to complete, was made by putting multiple ramps together.

According to many, it could take weeks—or even months—to master the ramp. Trainers put airbags in place on the ground as Brown started her training. After only three tries, Brown nailed it. She slid down the ramp, sailed through the air, and successfully stuck the landing!

FACT

In 1999, skateboarding legend Tony Hawk became the first person in history to land a 900. This is two-and-a-half midair full turns on the skateboard.

CHAPTER FIVE

OLYMPIC DREAMS

The Olympic committee announced that skateboarding would be added to the 2020 Tokyo Olympic Games. The Olympics are the biggest sporting event in the world and Brown set her heart on competing there. As usual, Brown's motivation was to inspire other kids.

"If they watch me skate or do this trick, they'll think maybe they can do it, too," Brown said. "That's why I want to do the Olympics—to inspire those kids who think they can't do it."

Because her parents are from different countries, Brown could represent either Japan or Great Britain in the Olympics. The Olympics are the biggest sporting event in the world. At first, Brown's parents were afraid the pressure would be too great. However, Brown's mom, Mieko, explained why they chose to represent Great Britain. "The team position for Sky was very relaxed," she said. This helped keep the pressure off Sky.

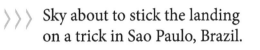
>>> Sky about to stick the landing on a trick in Sao Paulo, Brazil.

>>> Brown smiles for the cameras after taking third place in the Women's Final at the World Park Skateboarding Championships in Brazil in 2019.

Joining Great Britain's Olympic team was just the first step. Brown still needed to qualify for the Olympics. Due to the **COVID-19** pandemic, the Tokyo games ended up being delayed. Other skating competitions were cancelled too.

To pass the time during the pandemic, Brown stayed fit by creating workout challenges on her YouTube channel. She also supported *The Telegraph* newspaper's "Keep Kids Active in Lockdown" campaign.

In 2021, the 2020 Tokyo Olympic games went ahead as planned. Brown competed in the park skateboarding competition. Although she fell off her board on her first two runs, she landed all of her tricks in a flawless third and final run.

Brown placed third and became Great Britain's youngest Olympian to win a medal! With a bronze medal added to her achievements, Brown has her eyes set on the 2024 Paris Olympics. She hopes to compete in two events—skateboarding and surfing.

CHAPTER SIX

MORE THAN A SKATEBOARDER

Brown's dreams go beyond being a skateboarder. She is also a talented surfer who gets up at 5 a.m. to ride the waves with her brother. Brown is learning the guitar and enjoys writing her own music. She also takes acting and singing lessons. Brown also loves jujitsu and snowboarding.

〉〉〉 A 10-year-old Sky Brown riding the waves in Costa Mesa, California.

In 2020, Brown recorded her first song. Titled "GIRL," the music video features her skateboarding. It has more than 3 million views on YouTube.

That same year, Brown published a book called *Sky's the Limit: Words of Wisdom from a Young Champion*. The book is a collection of her inspirational quotes including the motto in which she lives by: Be brave, be strong, have fun, and do it because you love it!

FACT

In 2018, Brown competed on the television show *Dancing with the Stars: Juniors*. Although she had no dancing experience, Brown finished in first place!

THE SKY'S THE LIMIT

Sky Brown continues to inspire the next generation of athletes. Whether it's getting back up from a fall or trying something new, Brown does it with a positive attitude. Brown's number-one goal is to have fun, even more than winning. However, Brown is a champion at heart and will undoubtedly experience more wins in the future.

》》》 Sky Brown wins silver in a Tokyo Games Olympic qualifier in 2021.

TIMELINE

2008 Sky Brown is born on July 12 in Miyazaki, Japan.

2011 Brown learns to skateboard.

2013 Brown's skateboarding video goes viral.

2015 Brown competes in her first local competition and finishes third.

2016 Brown becomes the youngest skater to compete in the Vans US Open Pro Series.

2017 Brown finishes in second place at the Vans Park Asia Continental Championship.

2018 Brown wins *Dancing with the Stars: Juniors*.

2019 Brown finishes in third place at the World Park Skateboarding Championship.

2020 Brown suffers a serious fall from a ramp and recovers.

2020 Brown resumes skateboarding and releases a music single and book.

2021 Brown wins the bronze medal at the 2020 Tokyo Olympic games and becomes Great Britain's youngest Olympian to win a medal.

GLOSSARY

CONQUER (KAHN-kuhr)—to take control of something

COVID-19 (KOH-vid nine-TEEN)—a very contagious and sometimes deadly virus that spread worldwide in 2020

FOOTAGE (FU-tij)—a length of film made for television or movies

FRONTSIDE 360 (FRUNT-side three-siks-tee)—leaving the slope and turning 360 degrees before hitting the ground again

HEAT (HEET)—one of several rounds of competitions that determine which compeititors advance to the main event

KICK TURN (KIK TERN)—the process of riding up on a ramp or slope and then turning to ride back down

KICKFLIP (KIK-flip)—a trick in which a skateboarder flips the board over in the middle of a move called an Ollie

PRODIGY (PROD-uh-jee)—someone who is extraordinarily good at an activity at a young age

SIGNATURE (SIG-nuh-chur)—the move for which an athlete is best known for

UNCONSCIOUS (un-kon-SHUHSS)—not awake; not able to see, think, or feel anything

VEER (VIHR)—to change direction or turn suddenly

READ MORE

Brown, Sky. *Sky's the Limit: Words of Wisdom from a Young Champion.* New York: Penguin Workshop, 2020.

Kenney, Karen Latchana. *Extreme Skateboarding Challenges.* Minneapolis: Lerner Publications, 2021.

Prescott, Sierra. *Shredders: Girls Who Skate.* New York: Ten Speed Press, 2020.

INTERNET SITES

Kiddle: Skateboard Facts for Kids
kids.kiddle.co/Skateboard

SkateboardersHQ: Ride in a Day
skateboardershq.com/how-long-does-it-take-to-learn-skateboarding

The Boardr: Sky Brown
theboardr.com/profile/28691/Sky_Brown

INDEX

AUTHOR BIO

Cheryl Kim is an elementary teacher from California currently teaching at an international school in Thailand. She lives in Chiang Mai with her husband Brandon and sons Nathanael and Zachary.